A Daughter's Reflection

on the Suicide of Her Father

A Collection of Writings, Poems, and Narratives

Teresa Mohme

To Gloria Lloyd, for fulfilling her vision of a grief writing support group. Without her gentle nudge to join the group, my writings would still be frozen within my heart.

ACKNOWLEDGEMENTS

For their love and support during this devastating time in my life, I send out a heart-felt thank you to my friends.

A very special thank you to my sister, Pat, who motivated me to start working on this book sooner than I thought possible. Thanks mom, for taking two pictures that I'm sure you never imagined would make it into a book.

To Michelle Stauffer, Bob Seward, and Ruth Allaire for your constructive comments and corrections you marked on my work in progress. I deeply appreciate your time spent in helping me fine tune this beautiful book.

I am forever grateful to Susan Carter Morgan for her insightful editing and validation of this book.

To all those in the writing support group, the support group for grieving the death of a parent, the bereavement staff and volunteers at Mary Washington Hospice, a special thank you. They showed me that I was not alone in my grief. Their compassion, understanding, love and hugs gave me hope and courage when I felt at a total loss.

CONTENTS

Introduction
In Loving Memory

INTRODUCTION

I had stopped writing poems a long time ago. It never dawned on me to start writing again after my father's suicide. I felt totally lost. A friend suggested journaling. I quickly discovered that this was my way of keeping track of the day's events. I needed a constructive outlet for everything I was feeling. So lost, I could barely think straight. The unexpected loss, devastation, pain, sorrow and the question why were so overwhelming. I knew I needed to start putting back together the pieces of my broken heart, but where was I to begin!

I found a grief support group at the Mary Washington Hospice / Bereavement Department. Even though I felt immediately comfortable with the group, there was still something holding me back from reaching my deepest pain over my father's suicide.

The grief writing support group was started in January 2010, almost a year after my father's passing. It was through this group, that I rediscovered my gift for writing about my emotions. Since then, I have been writing about every weekly topic and then some.

The topics, I discovered, help me to stay focused, give my thoughts direction and motivate me to keep writing. I have included a list of our writing topics for those who may want to give writing a try.

In Loving Memory of Udell C. Mohme

January 30, 1930 - February 12, 2009

This book is dedicated to my father who, I have discovered, was truly my greatest teacher. Love never ends.

CHAPTER ONE

WHEN A LOVED ONE TAKES HIS OWN LIFE

The days, weeks, and months following dad's suicide filled with shock, denial, numbness and disbelief were almost too much to bear.

"The strength and power of action becomes inaction when not aligned with our hearts. We must do right things because it is right, for no other reason; then we stand in our power. Not for accolades from our friends or parental pressure, or even pressure from the dogma of the multitude of different faiths. We do this rightness from the direction of our hearts. This is power. Then we truly walk the beauty path."

Reverend LaKota One Heart

SELF-REALIZATION

That in death
  the living sometimes breaks from traditional norms
    either by choice or out of necessity for
      self-preservation.

I found myself back in two thousand and three
  breaking a long standing tradition by choice.

My grandmother who had lived a
  good long life for one hundred and one years
    had myself and her great granddaughter
      Christy help lay her to rest.

Six years later I found myself
  breaking from tradition in a much more dramatic
    way but this time it was out of necessity for my
      own self-preservation.

I could not continue to keep inside my grief, guilt,
  pain, and devastation I felt over dad's suicide.

I had to let it out through openly talking and writing
  about the traditionally taboo topic of death by
    suicide, I started my journey into uncharted
      territory.

What would people think about dad and me
  for that matter?

Breaking from tradition is not always easy.

But I soon discovered that the more I told
  my story about dad's suicide, the shame
    associated with his choice diminished.

I no longer cared what people might think.
  I was going to continue talking about this
    taboo topic.

For there is a healing power in the sharing
  of one's story.

No matter how painful it is at the moment
  of sharing, the moment passes quickly.
    Then the healing power begins.

*Society's unspoken "rules" is what I refer to
as tradition in this poem.*

SIX WORD MEMOIRS

Morning alive
   Home alone
      Afternoon dead

Morning alive
   Afternoon dead
      Note left

No goodbye
   Everyone heartbroken
      Total disbelief

ENDING - - BEGINNING

A song is sung
     A candle is lit
          A prayer is said
               for the departed.

Tears are shed
     Moans are heard
          As the casket closes
               on a journey ended.

A candle is lit
     A prayer is said
          Tears are shed
               Moans are heard
                    As the journey begins
                        without you.

BOUND BY AN IMAGE

Parallel grief, disbelief, and anger
  in a sight that no one should have seen.

Joins mom and I on a level
  which should not exist, but it does.

Dad timed this by his own desire
  so mom would not be alone.

The image that joins us - - - we don't talk about,
  a silent understanding exists.

When a reminder comes up
  we look at each other and in the locking of our eyes,
      there is a force that passes between us ......
          change the subject or the channel.

It exists and always will
  the bond that mom and I have
      in a sight, the initial shock, disbelief, and anger
          that should not exist.

But it does exist
  that which we don't talk about.

FIVE MINUTE TALK

Given five minutes, with the knowledge of what you
  were planning, I would have told you how much I
  love you, how much I need you, how much I
  look up to you, and everything you mean to me.

Even if it meant giving up my life in Virginia
  to help mom with getting you well, I would still
  love you.

I would have begged you to tell me how you were
  feeling. Why you felt you were heading towards a
  nervous breakdown. Why you felt that you weren't
  any good to us "this way."

Dad, how could you feel that you were no good to
  us? You mean the world to me. I love you
  unconditionally.

I have so much more to learn from you.
  I would be lost without you.
  I'm not ready to lose you to death before
  your time. Please do not take your own life.

How could you abandon mom, the woman who has
  been at your side, through thick and thin for
  fifty-seven years?

How could you abandon all those who love you
  and look up to you? What kind of example are you
  setting for those who love you unconditionally?

Had I known what you were planning
  I would not have let you out of my sight
    until you were safely in the care of
    professionals, willingly or by force.
  I would have made sure you got the help you
    needed because I love you.

SIXTH SENSE

When I went home in January to cheer you up
  and to be there when you got your doctor's results,
  on some level, I must have known that something
  would go terribly wrong.

Flying home never entered my mind,
  planning on staying only two weeks, I took my cats
  with me.

I packed one good outfit, my nice winter coat,
  everything I needed to make dream catchers and
  a month's supply of smokes.

When you said "I don't know what to do," I thought
  you meant, what to do with your time during the
  winter. I offered to teach you how to make dream
  catchers. You showed no interest.

Now I know you meant - you didn't know what to
  do about how you were feeling. My sixth sense
  failing to pick up on your despair.

I planned on wearing my nice outfit to celebrate the
  good news from your doctor, but you were not
  relieved by the news.

My sixth sense failing me once again, for I had no
idea I would need my nice outfit and my good
winter coat, to wear at your funeral.

My sixth sense caused me to be prepared to spend
more time at home, but failed me in matters of the
heart.

WHY ME

I had never bothered much with asking why, until
  your passing.

Your suicide note answered some.
  My spiritual teacher helped me understand other
  aspects on a much deeper level.

I still wonder why you felt there was no chance of
  you getting better.

Being born in 1930 and dying at seventy-nine, I'm
  sure you were raised not to talk about certain
  things.

Why didn't you trust us enough to help you?

Why choose me to help mom find you?
  You must have felt I was strong enough, that I
  would be level-headed enough and that I would be
  able to keep mom together.

LAST IMAGE REVISITED

Getting beyond the last image of how you committed suicide has been very hard, but getting past it I must so I can move beyond my anger and start the healing process.

At first I brought in the image of you sleeping peacefully as people passed by offering their condolences. I was still in denial, not wanting to believe you were gone.

As that last image continued to invade my mind I started calling in the image of the last time I saw you smile. The last hug you gave me, hearing you say, "I love you." Your laugh and your touch on my shoulder.

With the passing of time, whenever that last image comes uninvited into my mind, I switch that image to happier one's.

Going back further in time, to putting together our last puzzle, you're many smiles during past visits, doing projects together around the farm, until much to my surprise, I have started remembering more details about the good times we had together.

Sometimes when that last image just won't leave, I
   look through the photo album I put together of
   all the special times I spent with you.

Over time I've discovered that even though that last
   image will always be with me - - it no longer stops
   the images of happiness, joy, laughter, and fun that I
   shared with you.

BLUE BIRD PUZZLE

I will cherish forever, the picture of you and me
   putting together our last puzzle, an activity we
   always enjoyed doing together.

The puzzle was a picture of a quilted heart.
   Made out of a branch with leaves, a male and
   female blue bird perched upon the heart.

You insisted that we glue and frame it, but you never
   saw it framed. I wrote on the back; "I pray that you
   have found peace." "I love you and miss you,"
   signed and dated with tears in my eyes. It hangs in
   the room in which we put it together.

The heart easily broken; the universal symbol of love.

Your passing was in late winter, transitioning with
   the blue birds, with a broken heart not visible to the
   naked eye, leaving behind many broken hearts.

As I watch the blue birds this spring mending nests,
   happily preparing for a new batch of offspring,
   feeling fulfilled and at peace with their world.

I have to smile at how simply they view life.
They know only the seasons: not minutes, months,
  or years.
Heaven also is timeless.
My prayers for you finding peace within have
  already been answered.

Now my prayers are for all of us that were affected
  by your passing - all the broken hearts you left
  behind to find peace and forgiveness in their hearts
  so their mending, and my mending, can be . . . as the
  loving blue birds that brighten up my days.

SHATTERED DREAMS

You died before your time, by your own hand,
   shattering many dreams.

I was counting on you to show me how to grow old
   gracefully. For several years you did, after losing
   your sight in one eye, adjusting quickly you
   resumed the flying of your remote airplanes.

What happened to change your determination to
   make the best out of any situation?

Oh, the shattered dreams of learning more from you,
   having you to call on for strength and guidance,
   doing puzzles together and visiting with you and
   mom.

I must mention also, how you shattered moms
   dream of growing older with you. You broke your
   assumed promise, that you both would die
   naturally as close together as possible.

I wonder how many of your own dreams you
   shattered by taking your own life.

LEGACY

The legacy that dad left me was the beauty
  of having been raised on our small, family farm
  with the values inherent with this way of life.

Being care-takers of the land, hardworking with
  humility and patience, knowing I have no control
  over the forces of nature, but that observing and
  quiet contemplation, brings understanding and
  wisdom.

I would not trade this legacy for any other,
  but there is one part of dad's legacy
  I wish had never come to be...
  his choice to take his own life.

The human condition has a way of forgetting
  all the good, once someone makes a huge
  error in judgment.

Personally, I will change that condition
  by remembering all the good and placing his last act
  at the very end of his legacy
  as a period on the last page of his life.

WHO I WAS RIGHT AFTER DAD'S PASSING

Weighed down by the disbelief, pain and anger
the weight of the world seemed to be resting
on my shoulders.

Mom and others depending on me, the weight was
nearing unbearable intensity.

Walking around in a daze, indecision and
concentration flying out the window, when I needed
it most.

Rattled and scattered by the unexpected.
Emptiness settled in after my sisters had to leave.

I hid behind a mask of strength. Surviving by
determination, inner strength, and supportive calls
from friends.

Once I returned home, I was able to get back into my
usual routine. It worked for a while, putting dad's
suicide out of my mind, but the hardest part was
still to come.

Loneliness, isolation, despair and anger began
growing inside. With the support of my friends, I
knew I had to seek help in dealing with my grief.

CUT TO THE BONE

I used to think that only those who had also lost
  a loved one by suicide, could truly understand how
  deeply this act cuts to the bone, through it, and
  beyond.

Like a spear being thrust through your entire being
  from every angle until there is no part of you that
  hasn't felt the sharp edges.

Until one night I went to an all-purpose support
  group. After sharing my story of dad's suicide, a
  total stranger came up to me and very casually,
  without emotion or compassion, said "There have
  been several suicides in my family and it does run in
  families, you know." "It's just a mental illness."

My first impulse would have gotten me into trouble,
  so I just politely walked away. Anger was rising …
  how dare she say such a thing to me.

How could she be so callous not only towards her
  own losses, but to mine as well. Her words cut
  deep.

After finding a loving, compassionate, understanding and truly supportive grief writing group, I no longer think that only those who have lived through the suicide of a loved one, can understand the depth to which it cuts through to the bone.

All losses of loved ones to death, no matter what took their lives, have the same devastating effects on those who love them.

MY INNER CHILD

Searching deep within to find meaning and hope
   for my broken self, I discover my inner child.

Devastated beyond belief by your untimely death,
   caused by your own hand.

Even though my adult self has come to terms with
   and has forgiven you for your suicide, my inner
   child has not.

She does not understand, lost without her dad to take
   away the pain of her booboos, to hold her while she
   cries, and to tell her everything is going to be okay.

My adult self has no choice but to be father and
   mother to my inner child: holding, comforting, and
   trying to explain things in ways a child can
   understand.

Finding meaning and hope within my broken self
   has become a tougher challenge. For until my inner
   child forgives you, my adult self cannot continue to
   find hope, within the meaning of life.

WOULD IT BE DIFFERENT
HAD IT BEEN DIFFERENT

Had you died at one-hundred and one like your
 mother, I could have taken some comfort in the long
 life you had lived. Even though you were
 seventy-nine, you still had more good years to live.

Had you been dying from an incurable disease, I
 would have had time to write down the stories of
 your life, gotten answers to my questions, and tell
 you one last time that I love you. But then again, I
 would have had to see you suffer until the end
 came.

Had you died suddenly from a heart attack or an
 accident, at least I would have known why you
 died.

You chose to die by suicide. Even though you left a
 note, why will never really be answered.

Would it be different had you died differently?
 I think not, but you sure made it a lot harder on
 those who love you.

The devastation of your passing would have been enough, but because of your choice, we have major guilt, struggles with forgiving you, trying to forgive ourselves, dealing with the stigma associated with suicide and the ever-consuming why.

CHAPER TWO

PUTTING BACK THE PIECES...

*of my emotional and mental essence as I
navigate through uncharted waters of grief.*

"Spirit is the Life, Mind is the Builder and Physical
is the Result!"

Author unknown

FLOATING FEATHERS

Feathers floating in the void of my broken heart
  hearing the sounds they make within.

The pounding of raindrops on a tin roof
  drums a different heartbeat, with a quickening
  that increases the pressure within my broken heart.

How much more can my heart withstand…

How much more weight can it bear…

Feathers floating in the void
  lightly drifting through my broken heart.

Weaving the broken pieces back together
  with their quills and feather strings.

BROKEN FOUNDATION

You who have taught me so much
  with love, patience, and support.

The quietness, but firm presence
  of your physical body and mind.

All shattered in a moment.
  That which took a lifetime to build.

The foundation that was built
  upon your strength, love, compassion, and
  gentleness has been shaken with earthquake force.

How can I repair such a huge crack in a foundation
  that supports everything built upon it,
  without your help?

THE SHADOW

Falling within the cracks of despair
  only to find I am not alone,
  for the face of death lurks in the shadows.

Water floods the cracks of anger
  putting out the fire within.
    I float along with the current
    only to discover I am not the only one there,
    for the face of death invades the shadows.

I struggle with grief to find solid footing
  on the crack filled surface,
  only to find I am not alone.
    For the face of death sneaks behind
    within my own shadow.

INNER WORLD

After the storm had finally passed
  I look inside myself, finding layer upon layer
  of crumbled mortar, that once had held
  my inner world together.

Discovering this, a new storm came flooding in:
  the repairs could take a lifetime.
    Inner strength low, overwhelmed by the
    destruction that your suicide had caused.

With inner tears, I start remixing the mortar.
  Determined not to succumb to my pain and grief,
  finding my inner strength, my new foundation
  starts to hold.

With my inner world holding strong,
  I feel anchored enough to start putting back
  together the shattered pieces of my life.

JIGSAW PUZZLE

Devastated by the loss of a loved one, not knowing
  how I could possibly survive without you.

How does one grieve?
  The stages have been defined but,
  grief is not that simple.

To get through those first days and weeks
  I gathered up all the shattered pieces of my life
  threw them into a box, tucked away, out of sight,
  out of mind.

Once full reality hit, that you were gone forever,
  the temptation to lock the box containing all my
  shattered emotions: pain, sorrow, anger, despair,
  disbelief … and throw away the key - -
  was almost overpowering.
    I locked the box deep inside, keeping the key
    close by - just in case.

For a while I was able to keep the box hidden,
  not dealing with my grief.
    My anger towards you was ready to explode,
    I found the key and unlocked the box.

Putting back together the pieces that were shattered
  by your passing is like trying to put a jigsaw puzzle
  together, but without any picture on the box
  that shows what the final picture looks like.

Feeling overwhelmed - so many pieces. Each piece
  needing to find its place. What if I lost some?
    What if there are left over pieces?

I take a deep breath and search for a starting piece.
  I find two straight edges that fit my anger. I find
  more pieces that fit, not my anger but my sorrow.
    Now I know that each component of my grief will
    have its own picture.

With the realization that this process will take awhile,
  I close the box and move it closer to the surface of
  my being, unlocked with the key inside.

Each time my grief overtakes me, I revisit the puzzle
  box, finding more pieces to the pictures that is now
  becoming my life without you.

There is no easy way or quick fix for my grieving
  your death.

The passing of time and the slow process of putting back together the pieces of the jigsaw puzzle, will eventually lead me to a place where your passing fills my heart with more loving memories than sorrowful ones.

HITTING A WALL

In the beginning I hit a wall,
  invisible to my conscious mind.
    Like humpty dumpty, I shattered, barely able
    to piece myself back together again.

But here I am today - stronger than before.

I hit the invisible wall, put myself back together
  as best I could, with the empty space, that the loss
  of dad left forever a part of me.

This empty space projects the invisible wall,
  no longer invisible to my conscious mind.

For I have started painting pictures of memories
  upon this wall, so that helpless creatures
  will not fly into this hidden wall,
  saving myself and others from sudden death.

LOOSE THREAD

The tapestry of my life has a loose thread.

By pulling this loose thread, would I fully unravel or
  just the pain and sadness?

Would my emotions flow out in all directions,
  totally uncontrollable?

I wonder... by pulling this one loose thread, would
  the beautiful picture of my life good and bad
  be destroyed.

At which point would I stop the unraveling
  and start the tedious job of re-weaving the tapestry
  of my life?   Would I or could I make changes?

Dare I pull that thread to find the answers or
  do I just tuck the loose thread back into place
  and wait to see what happens next.

INTERNAL GHOSTS

Ghostly forms from within me
  fly out upon the full moon sky.

Raising the hairs of cats as they pass,
  scaring rabbits back to their dens.
    Even the bats fly up to the moon
    casting their shadows for all to see.

The ghosts of my mind need
  to find a new home, with all its guilt
  and should have known.

Setting them free with God's love
  will give them the light to follow
  so they won't stray to the unsuspecting.

Am I ready to free myself of these ghosts
  within my mind?

*The smallest detail within an object can bring
inspiration which leads to greater understanding.*

HORIZON OF BREATH

A glass orb sits in the windowsill
  that reflects the horizon upside down.
    It does not matter how I turn it,
    the reflection remains the same.

The flower within has defied gravity,
  as all living things do, by growing up
  towards the heavens.
    However, the horizon remains reversed
    from its natural state.

Before the flower was trapped within the glass orb,
  its releasing breath was captured in an air bubble,
  forever entombed within the orb.

I wonder if the breath I released after finding dad,
  is trapped within my own glass orb.

As I struggle to return to a horizon that is
  right side up, could the answer lie within
  my own entombed releasing breath?

DISPLACED

I have been moved from my usual place
  not in the physical sense, but mentally and
  emotionally displaced by your passing.

Being displaced has created so many challenges.
  Taking what seems to be an eternity, to piece back
  together my life, from the devastation of how you
  left this world.

I am making slow but steady progress towards a
  greater sense of peace, understanding, and
  forgiveness; no longer feeling displaced
  in the world.

WHO I AM NOW

I will always be my father's daughter.
  I still feel like a little bird, thrown out of the nest
  too soon; out in the cold to fend for myself.

Through the process of reaching out to strangers for
  help, I've discovered that I can be outgoing and
  talkative. My shy, quiet nature put aside.

Rediscovering the writer inside; renewed interest
  in my craft work; my creative mind has awoken
  from its hibernation.

My confidence and self-assuredness returning
  slowly. Working on repairing my foundation
  and discovering, my own anchor in this world.

I will always cherish the strangers becoming loving,
  supportive friends, ever expanding into a beautiful
  community.

Feeling the weight of the world on my shoulders
  melting away, a little less weight with each
  passing day.

The good days are slowly outnumbering the bad
  days, I would still like a child's hug from my dad.

Me and my dad.

CHAPTER THREE

GRIEF AND ITS REFLECTION

*No longer drowning in my devastating loss...
the reflection of my grief surfaces, giving me
strength to continue my journey.*

"Give sorrow words. The grief that does not speak
whispers the o'er-fraught heart, and bids it break."
William Shakespeare

THROUGH THE EYES OF OTHERS

We journeyed with mom right after a major ice
  storm. We never go to visit grandma and grandpa
  in the dead of winter.

We knew something wasn't right. As the days went
  by, we knew mom had suffered a serious blow.
People everywhere, crying, anger, sadness.

We did our best to comfort mom, always searching
  her out when the house was quiet.
Loud noises and lots of people scare us.

After we got back home, we had a new challenge:
  to support and give comfort to our mom, to help her
  through her sadness and grief.

We are up to the challenge, for we are cats ---
  our mom's unconditional loving companions.

I, the oldest, Willow, have the responsibility of
  helping mom write in her daily journal - - jumping
  up to give her kisses when I feel her mood has
  changed.

Zoe is responsible for helping mom with her daily
meditation and prayers, helping her to stay focused
and calm.

When we notice mom going in circles, with no
direction in sight, one of us will flop on the floor
demanding attention. She always stops - -
regrouping goal met.

Even though we can't talk her language, our purrs
and kisses lighten her heart. Accepting our "hugs"
of support, she shows her appreciation by more
petting and play time.

We still don't know how to help her when she tries to
cry it's so new that it still confuses us, but I just give
her my special look and kisses, then things seem to
be okay.

When mom needs an afternoon nap to regenerate,
we are right there, laying on her or close by.

In the evenings we help her space-out in front of the
television. Zoe sometimes beats me to mom's lap.
She looks up into mom's eyes and I see mom smile.
We like it when mom smiles. I patiently await my
turn in mom's lap.

I see grandpa come to visit us, especially in the evening. I stare up at the ceiling. Mom sees nothing there, but I think she is starting to feel his presence.

As mom has started having more good days than bad, we can do more bird-watching than mom watching, but we still keep one eye on mom, just in case we're needed.

INTENSITY OF THE STORM

The intensity of the storm surrounds me as I walk
   among the living. Lightning flashing all around,
   with thunder being felt but not heard.
I continue my journey unafraid.

The individual faces in the clouds become one.
   Growing with increased intensity, the flashes of
   lightning becoming as bright as a thousand moons.

The storm engulfs me; so close I can almost touch the
   flashes of light. Joining with the white lightning is
   blue, pink, and yellow lightning bolts dancing their
   dance together. I feel the rumbling thunder
   intensify, but I still hear no sound.

The intensity of my emotions, pain and anger over
   your passing, are becoming one with the storm.
Electrified by the one huge cloud, I release my own
   lightning bolts of many colors. The rumbling of
      thunder being heard but not felt.

The storm has subsided as I continue my journey,
   walking among the living.

LIFE EVENTS

Life events will cause a change in who we are.
  The more devastating the life event is the more
    impact it will have on us.

In a negative way or a positive way, it can also make
  us change our priorities in life, which can either
  hinder or help us.

We do have a choice as to which way we go.
  As we move along the course of life with its many
    twists and turns, sometimes we will hit
    a major road block.

Do we have the strength to break through and
  continue our course or do we give up and reverse
  our direction?

Do we embrace the negative by continuing our
  unwillingness to forgive? Or do we allow ourselves
  the same compassion given to others in a similar
  situation and forgive ourselves for all the would,
  could, and should haves?

Guilt can be all consuming. Things that we had no
  control over can generate a mountain
  out of a mole hill.

The mountain is called guilt and
   we are the mole that continues to allow
   the mountain to grow larger.

The stick of dynamite is forgiveness.
So light the fuse and take joy in the destruction
   of the mountain called guilt.

TREE OF LIFE

My inner tree of life is stripped clean.

My grief has caused it to become bare of the fruit
that nourishes my spirit.

With each affectionate memory, my inner tree of life
produces a new bloom.

As my loving memories grow in number, they
outweigh my grief, producing more blooms on my
tree of life.

New fruit grows. My inner tree of life is renewed,
nourishing my spirit once again.

Bob Seward

CHARACTER IN SOMEONE ELSE'S BOOK

There is a silent presence in the house, wandering
  from room to room. Its presence only realized
  when an unfamiliar noise scares the cats.

It enters a room, stops, with hands on hips, as if
  wondering why they had gone into the room,
  lost for a moment, then moves on.

I sit and stare, watching closely as this silent presence
  turns into a robot, moving with silent focus, going
  about the house doing things that needs to be done.

Time slips by and the robot stops. I wonder what it
  will do next. The robot stays idle for so long that I
  leave my watchful position.

As I look in the mirror,
  I realize that I had been watching myself.

EMOTIONAL ROLLERCOASTER

My emotional rollercoaster has a life-force of its own,
  swooping down at lightning speed.

My pain screaming all the way down and stopping
  inches from the ground.

As the next rise begins, a sense of panic builds
  in anticipation of what lies ahead.

Sharp turns filled with sadness, then another drop,
  trying hard to stop my beating heart.

With my heart in my throat, I scream out in anger
  awaiting the next sharp turn.

MASK THAT HOLDS MY TEARS

By drawing and naming my many masks, they were no longer mysterious elements of myself. Giving them substance helps me determine the root cause of their existence.

MASKS

My masks are many. They are my protectors,
 my shields, my deflectors.

All levels of my being have a mask.
 Some still serve me well others I hold in reserve…
  just in case.

Some I reluctantly let down, others I wish I could let
 go, but I have allowed them to grow too thick.

My heart has all levels of masks, sealing my heart off
 even to close friends and family.

The one that hides my tears refuses to lower its
 defenses… even when I'm alone.

There is a danger with some of the masks
 I have chosen to hide my emotional pain.

My challenge now is to regain internal control.
 Balancing my many masks; allowing my tears
  to flow at home alone or within the comforting
  embrace of friends and family.

APRIL: THE CRUELEST MONTH

April is the cruelest month; with all the renewed life
but spring has sprung. I still await the spring in my
step.

Everything is coming to life, new and green.
The sweet scent of the lilacs and wisteria.

Grandma used to have the most awesome wisteria.
It brings back memories of her house and the family
gatherings we used to have there.

She also passed in the dead of winter, just like her
son, my dad. I like to think that the new growth is
your combined effort.

The emptiness left by your passing has made it hard
to plant new flowers.

The daffodils I planted late last year in your memory
showed no signs of life. Then one day, as if you had
touched them, they were ready to bloom.

Three tall, strong blooms appeared marking the way
up my stairs to my front porch.

LIFE CYCLE OF MY GRIEF

Butterflies have a unique life cycle,
　from the eggs, to caterpillars, to chrysalis form.
　Where transformation into butterflies occur,
　emerging with delicate wet wings, solidified with
　movement and warmth from the sun.

Perils wait at each stage. The plant dies before the
　eggs hatch, killer wasps draining the caterpillars'
　life force. Parasites invade the chrysalis,
　　butterflies emerge with damaged wings, doomed
　never to take flight.

And so it is with my grief.
　My loving thoughts and good memories of dad
　　produce the eggs of healing.
　My heart with all of its pain, sorrow, guilt, and
　　anger, produces a jungle of plants only caterpillars
　　will eat. The eggs hatch easily in this environment.

The same perils wait … My negative thoughts
　produce the killer wasps. My positive, healing
　　thoughts protect them as they eat upon the jungle
　　of plants that is slowly overtaking my heart.

Deep within my heart the chrysalis are allowed their
　transformation to occur in a safe, loving
　environment.

No parasites can invade my heart of hearts.

Butterflies emerge with wet wings from the safety
  deep within. Passing through the jungle of plants,
  they must find the light of day. Some are consumed
  by renewed grief, cycling back through emotional
  pains, disbelief and sadness that I thought I had
  healed.

Some survive the perilous journey through the entire
  cycle, healing a small part of me with its beauty and
  freedom of flight.

Therefore, I write, to allow more of my butterflies
  to fly into the light of day.

HAPPINESS LIVES HERE

As the days grow shorter
  my thoughts turn to all the cherished days
  that I took for granted, believing that dad would
  always be there.

Shortness of step, movement slowing, as I sink
  into the loss.

Happiness used to live here.
  The house feels empty, even though mom is still
  living there.

Loving memories are all around.
  Working on mom's list of things that need to be
  done; things that dad used to do.

Do I see a hint of a smile on mom's face?

Happiness used to live here.
  Maybe someday it will again.

LIFE IS GOOD – LIFE IS NOT SO GOOD

Like pulling petals off a daisy
  he loves me - - he loves me not
  replaced with life is good - - life is not so good.

On any given day, pulling off petals
  I never know which one I will end up on.

When happy memories do not lead to sad ones,
  life is good.

When Father's Day commercials
  and cards fade away, life is good.

When the last image of dad stays at bay,
  life is good.

There should be more petals added to the daisy
  to include - - life is just okay.

CHAPTER FOUR

SPECIAL OCCASIONS

I needed to hear what dad would have said,
so I cleared my mind and let his reply flow
through my heart.

"Heaven days are new beginnings for those we love.
Reminders, although be it harsh, that this life is the middle
of our journey; not the end. I rejoice on your heaven day.
You are safely home!"

Jane Namist and Janice Broom

Happy Birthday Dad

I light a candle to honor your birth.

Your choices in life brought you and mom together.
Your choices together brought your daughters into
  this world, four in all, me being your second.

Choices in life not only impact one, but many.
The rippling effects from choices we make are
  infinite.

How I was raised and the choices you and mom
  made have made me who I am today.

The only choice you made that I would have wanted
  you to change, is how you chose to end your life.
It saddens me greatly that you could not see
  another option.

Even with your last choice, with its devastating
  ripple effect, affecting the choices your loved ones
  are faced with, I would not have wanted any other
  father. I'm proud to be your daughter.

Happy Birthday Dad.

Love, Teresa

WINTER BLUES

It's not the holiday season that is the hardest
  to get through.
It's what comes on the heels of celebrating
  a new year.

The dread of coming into a new year
  in the dead of winter, is the painful memories
  that January and February brings to bear.

January holds your birthday and wedding
  anniversary.

February holds your death by suicide.

There is no escaping the heartache
  that the dead of winter brings
  with the coming of a new year.

BURDENS OF LOVE

The burdens of love that we carry with us -

The eagles flight into the unknown heavens above
  through the clouds of many faces, comes back to
  earth as a mystic fog, rising again to meet the sun.

Each turn of events, leads to another
  the burdens of love we carry…

The fox swiftly runs into the rising sun only to return
  with the bats hunting insects, in the mystical hour
  between the setting sun and the rising moon with
  stars ablaze.

The burdens of love we carry,
  growing lighter as we come to realize,
  that without this burden, our lives would be
  unfulfilled.

FIRST YEAR OF FIRSTS

The first Father's Day I spent healing my spiritual
essence, still in denial of his passing.

The first time I needed his advice, I cried inside
because I could no longer call and hear his answer.
I felt empty, realizing his vast knowledge was lost.

Later it dawned on me that from him, I had already
obtained great knowledge. I just needed to have
faith in my abilities, that I now know reside deep
inside.

The first Thanksgiving and Christmas, I spent at
home with mom. I missed dad's presence,
expecting him to walk in at any moment.
I felt empty, the house felt empty.

The first time I returned to the place of dad's suicide,
doing a ceremony, I had been taught, I smudged the
area with sage, cleansing and clearing any
negativity. I sang a song honoring dad's life with
loving memories to help him on his journey.

In my later visits to this spot, I was able to feel his
presence, free of the trauma that had happened
there.

The first birthday, quickly followed by the first
anniversary of dad's passing. It was a very grief
filled two weeks. I lit a candle honoring his birth
and death. It helped to ease my pain and sadness.

I have come to realize that I need to continue to
recognize the impact that dad's suicide has had
on me, mentally, emotionally, physically, and
spiritually before true healing and acceptance can
occur.

FAMILY TRADITION

One of our family traditions is to play pinochle
   during holidays, family gatherings, or whenever
   we have enough players.

The first time we played without dad, it felt weird
   with someone else sitting in his spot. Dad had
   always kept score, no one wanted that honor.

At first mom was hesitant about playing, but once we
   all worked through our silent sadness, the joy of
   partaking in a family tradition took over.

We all ended up having a great time, talking,
   laughing and joking around.

I know that I felt dad's happy energy at the table.

FATHER'S DAY LETTER

Dear Dad,

    The last three days this year have been harder than last year on Father's Day. Everywhere I look there are reminders of how special dads are, and it makes me miss you more.

    Last year I was on a three-day silent spiritual retreat. Next year I will go back to doing that over Father's Day weekend as a way of honoring you and healing myself.

    I did buy a battery-powered circular saw and drill. I know you would have loved getting it as your father's day present. They both work great. I still can't saw a straight line with a circular saw. Is there a secret to it?

    I built a nice little stand, but haven't finished it yet. Not sure if I want it for books or little knick-knacks. Wish you were here so I could get some ideas from you.

    Mom sounded good when I called her on Sunday. She calls me on Wednesdays, and I call her on Sundays. So we are checking on each other.

    I repaired the bird boxes you made for me last month, I'll get them back up soon, I promise.

    Hope you enjoyed my singing the song I was taught to send memories to our departed loved ones.

    I love you dad. Remember that I forgive you. Happy Father's Day.   Love, Teresa

YOUR REPLY … FROM HEAVEN

Dear Teresa.

I'm sorry you are having a tough time with Father's Day. I miss you a lot, too. The song was beautiful and your writings are very nice. They help me understand the pain I caused by my choice. Please forgive me. I was not in my right mind. If only I could re-do that day…

Practice makes perfect with your new saw. I sure could have used it, especially with my shoulders giving me problems. Glad to hear that you and mom are staying in touch so often. I know she really appreciates it, and I do, too.

Keep up the good work. Thank you for your forgiveness. I know it's not easy. Things will get better.

Love You, Dad

WHO HAVE I BECOME

Some days I feel like a nut, some days I don't.

Some days I am eaten by squirrels; my outer shell
  being ripped apart by sharp teeth.
Other days I am eaten by worms; my insides being
  painfully and slowly dissolved away, rotting from
  the inside out.

This is who I was on dad's first year in heaven:
  isolated and vulnerable. It was the most horrific
  year of my life.

As the second year of dad being in heaven closes,
  I look in the mirror, finding more grey hairs and
  wrinkles. I see sparkles in my eyes that I haven't
  seen in two years.

Through the devastation of dad's suicide, I am more
  open in sharing with others, finding my voice in
  ways I did not think possible.

I am more forgiving, compassionate, and giving.
I have started putting up more family photographs.
My priorities about living life are beginning to
  change.

I am very thankful that this year was kinder that last
for who I have become, has helped me survive
another year without dad.

WINGS

On the wings of angels
  I fly up into the heavens.

Light as a feather, I sit upon the clouds.
  As time floats by, I have no sense of what
    I am waiting for.

Have I died and gone to heaven to join dad?

On the wings of angels
  I fly up into the heavens.

Light as a feather, I float down into my bed.
  Where I awake to find
    the feather above my bed
    has fallen upon my pillow.

CHAPTER FIVE

REMEMBERING…

Life on a small farm brings fond memories of dad and my family.

There are three things that remain ---
Faith, hope and love --- and the greatest of these is love.
1Corinthians 13:13
The Living Bible

REMEMBERING MY DAD

Not as the man who lost weight, looking like a
  skeleton of your former self.
Not as the man who didn't know what to do say.

Not the way mom and I found you on the day;
  you shattered our world and all those you loved.

These memories are still too vivid not to be my first
  remembering of you. The sadness, pain, disbelief,
  anger and grief is still too great.

Hopefully time will fade this remembrance to where
  Remembering my dad…

As a strong, handsome, vibrant, gentle man with eyes
  that shined. Who always knew what to say, even in
  silence. You had a force about you that was
  calming, radiating a sense of security to where, I
  always felt'safe and loved.

Most childhood memories still escape me.
What I do remember brings tears to my eyes.
  Two spankings - I'm sure I deserved more.
  Your concern and warm embrace when I fell down
    the stairs, landing on the kitchen floor while
    sleepwalking.

Getting Santa Clause to make a surprise visit to our
  window.
Going fishing, riding with you on the tractor and
  helping me fix my bike.

The joy I felt when you would give me a hug.
The happiness, security, and strength I felt from
  these hugs followed by the words I love you.
          I love you, too, Dad.

CONNECTING OBJECT

You left no time for me to tell you how much
  I love you.

It's hard at times to find a connecting object, since
  most of our connection was built on everything
  except material objects.

This brings me to the last thing we built together.
Eleven days before your suicide, we started putting
  a puzzle together.

We had put puzzles together in the past, being our
  thing to do, especially in the winter.
    I had no clue that this would be our last.

I now know why you wanted it framed;
  as a constant reminder of your love.
    -- With the quilted heart and the two blue birds
    -- One blue bird portrayed as a real bird
    -- The other having passed over into the quilt.

You send blue birds to my house, I know it's you
  because… there are more blue birds in my back
  yard than ever before.

I will greatly miss building puzzles with you.

The blue bird puzzle we put together.

THINGS I WILL NEVER FORGET

Going for rides on the tractor securely held
  in dad's lap.

Being allowed to play in the wagons filled with the
  years harvest, as long as I did not throw out any of
  the grain.

The times dad took me fishing, smiling proudly
  as mom took a picture of us with my first catch.

Riding along with dad and helping him as he worked
  a second job hauling milk.

Being taught how to stack bales of hay to maximize
  stability and capacity as we pulled bales out of the
  bailer mom was operating; maintaining our balance
  as we moved over uneven terrain.

As time passes by without dad, the more good times
  I remember - times I will never forget.

CLOCK TURNS BACK

Remembering is like time travel,
  turning back the clock to relive the precious
  moments bringing dad back to life within
  my heart.

Remembering renews the laughter, joy, happiness,
  and the love, also the pain and sorrow.

Accepting the bitter with the sweet
  my time travel machine holds the pictures of dad
  throughout his life, all the way to the bitter end.

If I could physically turn back the hands of time,
  I would go back to change the outcome.

Since this is not possible, I will continue my time
  travel, turning back the clock, remembering the
  memories, that brings dad back to life within my
  heart of hearts.

STAYING WITHIN THE LINES

Dad was a master of the straight line
  planting each field in perfect lines
  and in an instant, being able to tell if something
  wasn't straight as an arrow.

I would venture to say that he lived most of his life
  staying within the constraints of the straight line.

Later in life, he went outside the lines
  when he asked for a gold chain for Christmas.
He started to wear shorts and sneakers around
  the house and out in public.

I did not inherit his ability to see and make straight
  lines, even though I can color within the lines
  very well.

Instead, I started living my life outside the lines
  at a very early age.
Now, later in life, I am more balanced between
  staying within the lines and living outside the lines.

If you had met my dad......

IF YOU HAD MET DAD ON THE STREET

You would not know, with just a high school
  education, that he was a jack-of-all-trades and a
  master of most.

He was a self-taught welder, carpenter, electrician,
  plumber, architect, builder, concrete expert, farm
  equipment repairman, bulldozer driver, and tractor
  mechanic.

You would not know that he was a deep thinker
  who extensively planned out repairs and all projects
  he worked on. When he spoke, people listened.

A man of patience, who when pushed too far
  walked away from the person.
His anger of impatience did erupt from time to time
  especially with hard-headed livestock.

I am inclined to paint a picture of a total angel
  but no person is that perfect, not even my dad.

THE ATTIC

Every room in my parents' house has memories
  of dad's presence - from mom and dad's life
  together, to gifts we girls gave to dad and mom
  over the years.

There is one place within the house that holds
  the treasure chest of memories and family
  history. This place is considered the attic.

Within this attic is dad's baby crib, roller skates that
  mom and dad wore when they were dating,
  scrapbooks that contains cards from their wedding,
  and other memorabilia as their family grew.

The greatest gift the attic will eventually give my
  sisters and me are the daily entries mom made on
  her yearly calendars: records of weather, crops, and
  livestock.

The true treasure is that she also recorded personal
  events, capturing a unique picture of our family's
  daily life.

SEPTEMBER SONG

September begins the harvest of what was planted
  in the spring, hard work and determination,
  working long hours out in the fields.

Family time reduced, too tired to play cards
  or go on weekend drives. The crops take priority.

Soon all the hard work will be done.
Time to rest and regroup, playing cards in the
  evenings, being able to spend more time with dad,
  doing puzzles and other fun things, going for
  weekend drives in the country.

Never much time for vacations, but we had an
  abundance of quality family time.

Dad was always close by.

Now he is farther away in heaven, free from
  the physical pain from years of hard work,
  plenty of time to visit his brother and parents,
  and most of all - rest.

CHAPTER SIX

CONTINUING BONDS

Love never dies, which keeps the bond alive.
Strengthening the bond brings a special kind
of comfort that love alone cannot give.

"There is an invisible connection between
parent and child that remains, even after
death."   Author unknown

CONTINUING BONDS

Grieving your passing by trying to let go and find closure, I lost sight of the love that forever binds us together, for it is this same love that causes me such pain.

Without realizing it, I continued the bond with you:
- By keeping the father's day gift I got for you the year you died.
- By buying myself tools on the second father's day, which I would have given you.
- By doing maintenance and repairs that mom needs done on the farm.

Everything I build with your tools, every gourd bowl I make, every time I wear one of your jackets, is my way of strengthening my bond with you. These are just a few of the material things, I have no intention of letting go of.

The only closure I need is the strength to forgive you. The wound is healing, but it still bleeds at times. Through my writings, I continue to work on my closure of events surrounding your death and as a means of communicating with you.

You reply by periodically sending blue birds to the
   tree that shades the labyrinth I walk each day. They
   bring with them the memory of the last puzzle
   we put together.

I accept this "sign" as a reminder that you are
   always with me, that you hear my communications,
   and that your love is forever, as is mine.

CONNECTIONS

On a molecular level, half of my DNA came from
  dad. On the physical plane, I inherited dad's blood
  type, brown eyes, and slim build. These can never
  be forgotten, lost, or destroyed except through
  death.

Objects that connect me to dad that could be lost,
      destroyed, or stolen are such things as:
  His high school ring, the only letter he ever
    wrote me, and two toy trucks and toy bulldozer
    that managed to survive.
  Several belt buckles and knives that used to be his,
    and the tools he gave me through the years and
    that I continue to inherit from mom.

The material things are nice to have as easy memory
  jolts of dad and the times we spent together.

But it's the essence of honor, respect, integrity,
  humility, dedication and other qualities of my dad
  that was transmitted to me, unseen and unnoticed
  over fifty-five years, that truly connects me to him.

ACCEPTING BLESSINGS

Clouds floating by with such grace, forming faces
  and animal shapes, trying to tell their story.
Is anyone listening?

Do I feel blessed? Sometimes yes, other times no.
Am I worthy of such blessings? Maybe...

Blessing by choice, I should consider.
Why not accept the blessings being offered?
When I reject a blessing, I not only disrespect those
  offering but, also hurt myself by not accepting
  the blessing.

Filling the void that dad has left will never truly be
  filled, no matter how many blessing I accept with
  an open heart.

Only with loving memories of what we shared
  together, as a way of honoring his life, will help
  fill the void: a blessing to you dad.

The clouds tell their story, shedding their tears
  for someone, somewhere, has accepted their
  blessing, taking their message to heart.

Is anyone listening to the message the clouds have to offer?

POWER OF ONE LETTER

I found the only letter you wrote me
  exactly twenty-five years after you wrote it
  and exactly seven days before the
  one year anniversary of your passing.

As I read through all four pages
  I realize that it took great effort,
  being a new experience for you,
  hating the fact that this was your first letter to me
      …the one and only.

You told me about things going on back home,
  talking to me as your adult daughter.
Telling me about decisions you were weighing
  to see which option was best for the family.

Having saved your letter has allowed me
  to recapture a part of you that would have been
  lost forever.

Happy because I saved the letter,
  sad because I will never receive another.
Feeling empty when I thought I had lost your letter
  when earlier attempts to find it failed.
Now I'm filled with your happiness and love,
  in sharing a part of you with me.

The timing was no coincidence.
You wanted to remind me just how much
  you loved me.

Saying that you hoped this letter found me
  well and happy, and signing it Love, Dad.

SPRING

Spring is when flowers and trees mysteriously
  come to life after appearing dead all winter.

You will never spring back to life.
As much as I want it to be so, I know it is not
  possible.

I look through my sadness to smell the sweet scent
  of spring, to taste the rain off fresh mown grass,
  to see the rainbow colors of spring.

The memories of you out in the fields plowing
  and working the land to receive seeds for new
  life, comes to mind.
There is no sweeter smell than that of a freshly
  plowed field.

Even though you are no longer physically in this
  world, your essence is everywhere –
  in each new flower, in each new leaf, in every dot
  of pollen, and within each drop of rain
  that makes a rainbow.

DAD'S PRESENCE

Walking into the building where you took your life
wasn't too hard since I had done it several times
before.

This time was different because I had chosen to build
a step for the family dog around the worktable
where mom and I had found you.

I could have chosen five other places, but I felt called
to build something here.

At first the last image of you came to me, but it
quickly disappeared as I focused more on seeing
you building things on your worktable.

I felt your presence as I started measuring and
cutting.
You told me I should be using a different saw.
I told you it was hard enough finding what I found,
not knowing your system of what tools were in
what building.

You also told me I should "square my cuts."
Your perfectionist side coming through loud and
clear. But I said, it's only a step for the dog, that
was going to be covered.

I felt at peace in this place where so much pain had resided.

Your presence, being at peace, knowing that I could get beyond that last image of you, and connect with you...

lifted my heart to nearly breaking, with love and happiness.

LETTER OF CONVERSATION

Dear Dad,

I miss you so much. I know you knew that I loved you. I wish I would have said it more. Thanks for being the best dad a kid could ever have. You taught me so much that I will always be very grateful for. You are always with me.

I am proud of you for seeing the wisdom in teaching me things that are traditionally taught to boys back in the fifties and sixties. Your teachings have come in handy. It has helped me be the person I am today.

I do have a few requests however. Since you have no limitations where you are now, could you please help mom sleep better, let her know that it's okay to smile, laugh, and have her moments of happiness. Talk to her in dreams, for she misses you dearly.

The other request is I would love to hear from you in my dreams. You have come several times, but I don't remember you saying anything. Help me to remember childhood memories.

Everyone seems to be doing okay. I missed your presence when, over the course of May, everyone was back together.

Love,
Teresa

YOUR REPLY BACK

Dear Teresa,

I will try my best to honor your requests, but I'm not sure how easy it will be with your mom. She can be very hard-headed at times and convincing her to be happy and laughing will take time and great work, probably a miracle or two.

I'm proud of you for doing all the work you did and helping mom take care of things, driving her places and noticing the car's oil pressure light.

I am truly sorry I put you in the position I did. I am proud of you. You did and are doing a great job.

I am also sorry that the stress had gotten to you and that you needed to seek help. I wish I had had your courage.

Hang in there, my sweet daughter. Remember that I am always with you.

Love,
Dad

SMILE IF I DARE

Smile if I dare
　　at the sorrow in my heart
　　　　for dad is gone but yet lives on.

Smile if I dare
　　at the devastation his death left behind
　　　　for dad helps me rebuild.

Smile if I dare
　　when helping mom with her grief
　　　　for dad sends me words to say to her.

Smile if I dare
　　when I have bad days
　　　　for dad is always watching over me.

Smile if I dare
　　at the love in my heart
　　　　for dad will always smile back at me
　　　　　　from heaven.

HEARTBEAT

The steady drops of moisture from my house
  drums out two distinctive heartbeats.

As with my parents, the two drumming heartbeats
  come very close to becoming one however, they
  retain a small part of separation.

The first heartbeat I heard was my mother's
  while awaiting my birth.

The second heartbeat I heard was my dad's
  who lovingly held me in his arms after I arrived
  in this world.

As I search to reconnect to my dad's heartbeat
  no longer physically present, I find it as a small
  separation away from what I recognize as mom's
  heartbeat.

The steady drops of moisture continue to drum
  two distinctive heartbeats.

I feel the drumming deep inside, and I know that
  my heartbeat lies somewhere in between.

WALK WITH ME

Walk with me as I journey through this maze of grief.
  So different from the labyrinth I walk each day
  where there are no dead ends or choices to make
  along the way.

As I journey through this maze of grief –
  walk with me. As only you can keep the tricksters
  away; moving way too fast for me to see.

Which turn should I make next - - I have no clue.
  So much pain and sorrow . . .
  way too many choices to make along the way.

I know you walk with me,
  as I journey through this maze of grief,
  for I feel your presence with each step I take.

Labyrinth

CHAPTER SEVEN

COPING WITH LOSS

Being of nature - - becoming one with nature soothes my soul ... giving me inspirational empowerment to carry on without you.

"It is truly rare that a person can share
the dimensions of grief in such a vivid way."
Ruth Ann Allaire

A NEW DAY

After starting this journey to reconnect
  with my emotions, through my writing
  and poems

My eyes have been opened, along with my heart
  to the beauty that surrounds me every day.

Today at pre-dawn
  crows flew in to hold "council"
  in a tree that was lit by the full moon.

As the sun began to rise,
  the moon vanished behind fog-like clouds.

The crows became silent, their council completed.

With their instructions for the day,
  they flew off in different direction,
  as night gave way to a new day.

ONCE UPON A SEPTEMBER NIGHT

On the third night of September
  a crescent moon glows bright orange
  in the western sky.

An owl calls out in the dead of night, waiting …
  but no call is returned.

The peaceful solitude of the third night of September
  is disrupted by a flurry of sound, from a celebration
  of fireworks, somewhere in the distance.

As the smoke drifts by, a flock of geese take flight.
Calling out to one another, ensuring a safe journey
  in the dead of night.

As time passes, the third night of September returns
  to quiet solitude.

With nature's lullaby, I drift off to sleep.

As I float into dreams, I can't help but wonder:
  what dad sees and hears as he looks down
  from heaven, on this third night of September?

OCTOBER'S BLANKET

October lays down her blanket of many colors
  for those who will snuggle underneath, as they
  slumber through the approaching winter.

Floating upon the crisp morning air is the increased
  chatter of birds, with geese adding their voices from
  high above.

An undercurrent of excited energy is felt by all.
In a flurry of activity, butterflies converge on the
  last remaining flowers of summer.
Squirrels frantically gather food, leaves for bedding,
  and secure their nests.

All the day's activities will soon give way
  to the silent falling of the leaves.

As October continues to lay down her blanket
  of many colors;
  softly covering those who have been laid down
  for eternal slumber.

FALLING LEAVES

Leaves of many colors drift down to the water below,
  like little boats carrying memories of you, to you,
  following the path the full moon shines upon the
  water, to beyond the beyond.

Rainbow colors belong to the sky, but the awesome
  fall colors belong to earth mother.

Only through the falling of the leaves, can the colors
  of our tears find expression.

Reds, oranges, yellows and browns, with all realms
  of colors in between.
The leaves falling, swirling, drifting upon the winds
  current of memories within doing the same.

As the last of the falling leaves float down, the trees
  become skeletons upon the landscape of life.

That which is born of earth mother returns to her
  to be recycled and born anew.

TAPESTRY OF LIFE

All throughout our lives we weave a tapestry --
a creative and unique picture of our lives.

Each event happy or sad, earth shattering or joyous,
good or bad, impacts the fabric of our lives
forever recorded upon this tapestry.

My tapestry has a huge area that is void of lively
color. The weave that I created when you
permanently left my life. Patterns of despair, the
weave so twisted and tight, that no light can shine
through.

As I move through my cycle of grief, new patterns of
color are weaved where happy memories reside.
Spring flowers emerge and fields are planted with
seeds; creating summer scenes of plants growing
to maturity.
Fall colors appear in my tapestry as harvest nears.
The cycle of life goes on despite the fact that you
ended yours.

I choose not to dwell within the colorless weave of
my life. Instead, I choose the artist within that can
create vibrant patterns, in the fabric of my life
with loving memories of you, as the cycle of my life
continues on.

ABSENCE IS A HOUSE SO VAST

Before I moved into the house that I live in now
  you could literally walk through the walls,
  feeling its vastness without barriers.

There was an overwhelming sadness that was
  bleeding out of every corner of the lifeless house.

My friend's father had never completed the house
  her mother had so hoped for. Both died, leaving the
  vastness of the house to continue bleeding.

As I moved in, I incorporated their furnishings into
  mine. The house became alive, the sadness gone,
  the bleeding stopped.

When my father died unexpectedly, the house picked
  up on my sadness. As I wandered aimlessly, from
    room to room, the vastness without barriers came
    crushing back.

I needed to stop the house from bleeding anew and
  sinking down into a deep sadness that no one could
  reach.

In my mind's eye, I started closing off the vastness
   with new walls that defines the space within,
   giving it depth and character with memories of us,
   as daughter and father.

Moving from room to room
   rebuilding the walls that define us,
   not as barriers to my grief, but as an honoring
   for my absent father.

Pictures of happy memories now hang on the
   walls and each room holds memorable objects.

My absent father is always with me
   and in his physical absence
   I continue to be, and always will be,
   his daughter that misses him deeply.

LONELINESS

The beauty that surrounds, brings pictures of
  remembering into my being.

Seeing a single tree through a forest of many
  one stands alone.

Supported by the others, but still alone, lost in the
  crowd.

Alone but not for long, as light shines through
  the lone tree is warmed by the embrace of the sun.

The loving warmth melts the loneliness away
  branching out towards others in the forest, filling
  the gap within.

Reaching up to return the loving embrace,
  the lone tree is no longer lonely. It feels whole,
  complete, alive, and able to support life within its
  branches.

No longer will the lone tree feel lonely or lost in the
  crowd. For it has regained its strength to take on
  the world once again.

OWNERSHIP

Do I own my emotions? If I do, how do I reach
   down to where my deepest emotions live
   to find the answer?

There are layers upon layers of emotions that I never
   dealt with from childhood, through young
   adulthood, to the present.

Do I claim these emotions as my own, or do I blame
   others?

Seeing is believing or is it believing is seeing?
I choose believing is seeing, for if I believe I can see,
   I will see what I need to see.

Looking through the hourglass, as time runs out
   upon the sandy beaches. Wave after wave taking a
   little more sand out to sea, to be cleansed or
   deposited elsewhere.

Sands of time return to the beach.
Emotions run deep within the ocean of my being,
   some cleansed, some washed away, yet others rise
   again without warning.

One layer at a time, seeing what I need to see.

I do own my emotions.
Realizing that at the moment in time when the
  emotions were felt, I did the best I could
  within that hourglass of time.

The winds whisper of hope and faith.

WINTER WONDERLAND

The tormented winds are constantly changing the
  landscape. Snow drifts appear in unlikely places.

Birds change their flight path, briefly fighting the
  tormenting winds, then quickly turning, letting the
  wind drive them to their final destination.

Within the agonizing winds is a whisper of hope
  and faith, so faint that one must listen closely
  to hear its song.

Struggling against the winds of torment only wears
  us down, giving up the fight, getting stuck where
  we stand, forced backwards to hence we came.

The winds of change need not haunt us.
The snowdrifts are only temporary hurdles to
  overcome, which the winds will move and change
  the landscape once again.

We need only to intensify the whisper of hope
  and faith, within the tormenting winds, reducing
  our fear of change.

Though the landscape is constantly changing and the drifts appear huge, our path can be found by briefly fighting for forward momentum, then using the whisper within the tormented winds to drive us to our destination.

HOLE IN THE WALL

A window is just a hole in the wall.
Through this hole the entire room is filled with
  light.

As I stare out of this hole, with blinds open wide,
  the walls disappear; seeing only the light shining in.

The light hits certain objects, filling my room with
  rainbows dancing all around.
Shadows playing hide-and-seek, as the light grows
  brighter with blinds opened wide.

This light brings rainbows into my life, to nourish my
  body, mind, and spirit, to brighten my mood with
  blinds wide open.

They say that through our eyes, our soul can be seen.
Is this not just a hole in the wall of our defenses,
  allowing our entire being to be filled with light?

Some wear blinders to hide behind so others cannot
  see inside.

Deflecting the light, with blinds closed to the world
  outside, trapping the darkness inside, growing
  doom and gloom.

I cast off my blinders,
   no longer needing or wanting the growing
   doom and gloom of the darkness inside
   that your passing has left within my soul.

The light fills my soul with dancing rainbows
   all around, shadows playing hide-and-seek,
   the light grows bright with blinds opened wide
   and I am filled with a willingness to live again.

INVINCIBLE SPRING

Introspection or hibernation
  in the depth of winter hibernation is easier.

Going through my days, fighting back the dark mood
  that winter brings with its gray, cold sunlight.

Introspection is the tool I use to wage war on the
  depth of winter. Sometimes I win.
    Sometimes I lose.

When I take the time to look within, I discover things
  I want to change and need to change. I discover
  creative ideas and ways to grow beyond the
  devastation of dad's passing, in the depth of
  winter.

Most of my creative ideas I bring to fruition
  throughout winter as part of my arsenal against
  the darkness, that is winter.

The rest I plant within my invincible spring, to
  nurture with love and tenderness until strong
  enough to drink the rains of spring. Beginning its
  growth towards fruition by springing forth buds
  under the warming sun.

During the depth of winter, my body lives for the warmth of summer, but my soul lives on the invincible spring within.

ONE STANDS OUT

There is a tree within a forest of many,
  that is unlike any other.

For it has a perfectly round hole through its trunk;
  four feet up from where it first put down its roots.

Above the see-through hole, its trunk continues to
  grow solid and straight as it reaches up to touch
  the sky.

The perfectly round hole, the size of a cannon ball,
  shot through the heart of this beautiful tree, as the
  Civil War raged within this forest of many.

Lives were lost, many wounded, hearts and
  landscape forever changed.

In the mist of it all, a tree survives with a hole
  through its heart. Growing beyond its injury with
  its wound forever remaining, a see-through hole.

We too can grow beyond our shot through the heart,
  by the loss of our loved one, with the knowledge
  that the hole in our heart will always be a part of us.
Healing can still happen around and above our
  wound, if we allow it.

STAMP ME FRAGILE

They say that time heals all wounds.

Do I have enough time to heal from your death
  before the next tidal wave hits?

No one will come to save the day.
Outward form looks strong.
But it is what's on the inside that has become,
  and still is, fragile.

Should I stamp my forehead with a message
  that says, Fragile - - handle with care?

They also say that we are hardest on ourselves,
  so maybe I should have fragile written on my
  mirrors, as a reminder to be gentle with myself.

THE UNEXPECTED

Even though I had twenty-four hour notice
  that the power company was going to cut down
  some trees and trim others, I was still floored by
  the devastation they left behind.

Gone were the trees, along with the beautiful cedar
  tree that marked my driveway.

Bushes trampled and the tall, beautiful pine tree
  without limbs on one side.

All the feelings came rushing back, as if dad's suicide
  had just happened.

Great pain and sadness swirled around me,
  through me.

I once again felt out-of-balance with one-half
  of my parental support gone, my foundation shaken
  once again.

They left the pine tree to struggle with its loss.
  As I too, struggle with my loss.

THE FRUITS OF LIFE

With each thought of sorrow, emptiness, and anger,
  a fruit on our tree of life drops off.

With each affectionate memory, a bloom grows,
  producing a new fruit upon our tree of life,
  renewing the cycle.

As our loving memories grow in number,
  more fruit is produced upon our tree of life.

Then in times of renewed sorrow, emptiness, and
  anger, we can pick a memory off our tree of life
  and once again be renewed.

Bob Seward

CHAPTER EIGHT

GRIEF AND TIME...TIME IN GRIEF

Grief has no time limit. The burden of grief has gotten lighter. My pain, anger and sorrow have decreased. The sense of loss will remain forever. Through it all, I will always remember my dad with great fondness.

"Nothing in the world is permanent or lasting;
Everything is changing, momentary and unpredictable."
Bukkyo Dendo Kyokai
<u>Teaching of Buddha</u> 1966

END OF THE VALLEY

From the outside looking in,
  the lonesome valley
    has no beginning or end.

Filled with thoughts and emotions
  as random and unique as snowflakes
    falling from dark winter clouds.

One could easily get forever lost,
  within this lonesome valley
    that only I must face
      stumbling through
        with down cast eyes.

GOOD-BYE

Saying good-bye seems so final,
  like saying the end and closing the book
  never to be opened again.

As a way of saying farewell, I choose to use
  bye, later, or see you later.
These feel less final, with the possibility
  of seeing them again.

Not saying good-bye to my dad's body
  in my mind is a moot point –
  for he is no longer there.

Some may say this is denial of his passing,
  but I do not deny that he died.

However, he lives on in so many ways,
  within his daughters, grandchildren,
  great grandchildren, dreams and memories.

To his soul I say "fair winds and following seas"
  for our paths will connect, at some point in time
  once again.

TIME

Time changes all things, if I don't change
  the only thing time can change,
  is everything that exists around me.

I become stuck in a time
  which becomes the past for everyone else.

I cannot know what time has in store for me,
  if I remain stuck in the past.

For time to heal all wounds, as the saying goes,
  I must change as time changes,
  going with the flow of life,
  healing through forward movement.

Creating vibrational changes within,
  becoming synchronized with time itself.

GRIEF RIDES WITH ME

Grief rides with me, but I am at the wheel.

Not content just to ride along, it also walks with me.

Not necessarily reflected upon my being,
  but it is there - all the same.

Sometimes I set the cruise control on my life,
  not wanting to deal with what tomorrow will bring.

Other times I cruise to give myself a break from the
  past, that which I have tried to leave behind.

I maybe driving my life, but grief rides with me
  and if allowed, could easily become the driver.

LONG PROCESS

In this day and age of instant gratification
  instant messaging, communication, instant news,
  notification, and bill paying…

It is no wonder that so many people think that
  grief can be fixed within weeks.

They say "suck it up and get back to living."

Obviously they have yet to lose someone they truly
  love or have become so calloused, they have lost
  their compassion.

WHERE IS "OVER IT"?

"Over it" may only exist in the minds
  of those who say, get over it and move on.

So where is "over it"?
  Is it in heaven?
  Is it in hell?

Grief can feel like one is going through hell
  so maybe it is on earth?

Fond memories can bring a sense of heaven
  back into our lives.
So maybe heaven is also on earth?

Bringing a little bit of heaven
  into each day of my life,
  is better than dwelling in hell.

Where is "over it"?
It remains a mystery.

GRIEF IN MY REAR VIEW MIRROR

In its own time most of my grief will be behind me,
  tagging along in my rear view mirror,
  but never disappearing over the horizon.

Most of the emotional intensity I felt following your
  death is behind me.

But the devastation your suicide left behind lingers
  in my side view mirrors.

After the second year passed without you, more
  elements of my grief have moved into my rear view
  mirror.

Forgiveness and acceptance ride close behind, but
  the destruction still lingers in my side view mirrors.

I can only hope that in time, the devastation that still
  lingers in my side view mirrors, will eventually
  move to my rear view mirror.

The empty space in my heart,
  the missing your presence in my life, will always
  remain as I go forward in life.

FROZEN IN TIME

Waterfalls frozen in time,
  suspended from rock cliffs.

Some hold the face of old man winter
  others hold a single lighten bolt.

Rays of sunlight shine through
  slowly releasing the tears of pain and sorrow,
    only to refreeze again with harsh reality.

As time passes,
  the cycle of release and frozen reality
    makes the frigid waterfalls smaller.

Until there is nothing left
  but a pool of water that reflects
    the face that once was.

WITHOUT A CARE

A leaf moves across the frozen canal
  by a force unseen.

It has no fear of falling through
  so light without a care,
  free of excess baggage
  it remains light as a feather.

It does not care if it is moving with or against
  the current beneath the ice.
Only the fish below know the answer.

More leaves catch the unseen force,
  skating their way upon the frozen canal,
  dancing their dance, without a care.

How I wish that, just for a moment,
  I could feel total freedom;
  to dance with the leaves upon the frozen canal
  without a care.

HOMELESS SOUL

Tumbleweed of emptiness
  no roots to hold it in place,
    riding the currents of the wind.

Its homeless soul collides with everything
  that the wind decides it should encounter.

No mercy is shown to the tumbleweed of emptiness,
  until it collides with a fast moving vehicle;
    shattering the tumbleweed into a million pieces.

No longer at the mercy of the wind,
  the shattered tumbleweed of emptiness,
    no longer homeless in its soul
      as it continues to get ground back into the soil
        of earth mother, finding its roots once again.

JULY AND INDEPENDENCE

July brings with it the second half of a year
    that has already gone by too quickly.

Maybe that is a good thing,
    instead of time lingering on in agony.

Trying to find a balance between living life to its
    fullest and my grief over dad's suicide,
    without his loving support, strength, and wisdom.

That which was born, hatched, or sprouted in spring
    continues its growth in July, the first full month
    of summer.

Young squirrels play chase, jumping from branch
    to branch.
Young birds test out their wings.
Fawns can now walk beside their mothers, no longer
    needing to hide.
Ducklings no longer need to follow behind; having
    learned all about being a duck from their mother.

As I look out upon the landscape of life,
    a sea of vivid, sparkling colors from all the summer
    flowers greet me.

Adding to the vibrant skyline of life, are beautiful
butterflies, dragonflies, and birds of many colors.

I still cannot declare my independence from grief,
but I can celebrate the beauty that surrounds me.

I invite you to journey down the path of writing with me.

WRITING TOPICS

My grief is like _____

Feeling numb in the middle of a huge tornado

Wish I knew then, what I know now

He/she isn't here, but he/she isn't gone

What would _____ say about _____

Feeling a presence in the absence

Unexpected triggers

How in my grief am I addressing my own mortality?

Absence is a house so vast that inside you will pass through walls and hang pictures in the air

Can we find meaning and hope in a broken self

Untold story

Letting go of the future that didn't happen

Letting go of things that once were, and can never be

Conversation with loved one

Would of, could of, should have

When grief takes you unexpectedly - - - blindsided

September song

Object that connects us to our loved one

Loss makes artists of us all as we weave new patterns in the fabric of our lives

Cut to the bone

Good bye

Falling leaves

Home or in the attic of my brain

Ghosts

First year of firsts

This sure takes a long time

Legacies

Hole in the wall

Good Samaritan

Consider this window, it's nothing but a hole in the wall but because of it the whole room is filled with light

Persona that we push part of ourselves into

Continuing bonds

Unexpected self-discovery

Who is this person / stranger I've become

Object that tells a story - - write the story

Something I'll never forget

As if the clock somehow turned back

Burdens I carry

Where is "over it"

To feel the sun on my back

Hitting a (the) wall

Pieces and parts

Would it be different had it been different

I thought I would go in a different direction

Standing at the edge of the cliff

Plan B {when Plan A no longer works}

Will I ever see grief in my rear view mirror?

Lonesome valley {old spiritual song]

Yes to life

July

Moving or intensity

Displaced {person}

Looking at life through a difference lens

Staying within the lines - - or not

Life as a temporary event

September

Transition

Deafening silence

Releasing the "genie" within and getting to the magical person that we are

Lost and found

Something I cannot forget

October

Un-played melodies of our lives

Empty places - found you in my heart

Giving thanks

How can emptiness weigh so much

December

Essence of loss

Start where you are

Four-leaf clover

What tastes sweet

Savor every memory / moment

My last words to you upon my death

Who I was

Who I have become

Who do I want to be

Why

Shattered dreams

Sixth sense

Inner world

Loose thread

Feeling as though I'm a character in someone else's
book

Reflection

April

Through the eyes of others

Masks

Blessings

Loneliness

Ownership

Who decides

Empty boardwalk

A completely different challenge

How do I manage grief?

Shelter from grief

Crossing the river

Life is not the same

Painful comfort

Dreams as guides

Smile again

Made in the USA
Charleston, SC
09 August 2012